EMPOWERING AFFIRMATIONS FOR BLACK WOMEN

POSITIVE AFFIRMATIONS TO INCREASE CONFIDENCE, BOOST SELF ESTEEM & MOTIVATION AND ATTRACT SUCCESS FOR BADASS BLACK GIRLS

ALICIA MAGORO

If you would like to review this book, please scan the QR-code with the camera on your smartphone.

This will take you directly to the review page.

Or type in the Shortul link below in your web browser.

shorturl.at/EZF59

CHAPTER 1

INTRODUCTION

Are you a Black woman with a desire to lead an amazing and fulfilling life?

Are you tired of being subjected to stereotypes that tend to clip your wings?

Do you desire happiness, confidence, and positivity in your life? Then this audiobook is for you.

There's no overstating that there are challenges and stereotypes you have to face as a Black woman. Unlike everyone else, you don't get to start on a level playing field. You are judged, misjudged, and written off even before you say a word. All of these culminate in a depressing and lackluster life. You almost feel like giving up and accepting the mediocrity life throws at you.

Not so fast!

You deserve a happy life. You deserve a rewarding, fulfilling, and enriching life. Like everyone else, your dreams are valid, and you have to pursue them. But it all starts in the mind. Your mind holds the truest power to transform your life. That's why you need positive affirmations.

Positive affirmations are widely considered to boost confidence, mood, and self-esteem. Through the incredible power of repetition, you're able to reconstruct the thought patterns, beliefs, and ideals in your subconscious mind. That way, you set yourself up for the wonderful life that you desire.

WHAT ARE POSITIVE AFFIRMATIONS?

Your ability to stay positive, to use positive words determine the tone of your emotional life. Positive affirmations are words that speak positively about your life, emotions, career, and everything else.

Basically, you are saying what you want to see, regardless of the prevailing circumstances. Affirmations are more than just simple words you speak; you go a step further to identify with them. Simply put, these words become your own. They become your ideals and frame your belief systems.

These positive statements help you overcome negative thoughts that trap you in an endless cycle of pain, pity, and unproductivity. When you repeat them often enough and actually believe them, you can start to make the necessary changes in your life. In that lies the secret of affirmations: you have to keep saying them.

Some people consider positive affirmations as a waste of time. Others call it merely wishful thinking. But if you look at them the way you consider physical exercises, you'll realize it portends far more value than we can even describe. In this case, you're exercising your mind for a positive outlook towards life. Think of positive affirmations as mental exercises that reprogram your mind.

HOW DO AFFIRMATIONS WORK?

In the simplest of terms, thoughts influence feelings, and feelings dictate behavior. So, if your mind is constantly filled with negative thoughts, the result will be a negative behavioral pattern. For example, if you think you can't be the best at work, you'll never put in the hard work and excellence that'll shoot you to the very top. The reason is simple: you've already lost in your mind.

The mind is a battlefield, and you have to win over your thoughts constantly. Positive affirmations help you reprogram negative thoughts into positive ones. The results might not be instant. But over time, you begin to notice a change in your thinking pattern and ideals. However, it doesn't stop there. The ultimate goal is that you start to manifest the affirmations into reality. That's when you begin to enjoy the benefits of positive affirmations.

The words we speak are significant as they directly impact how we behave. If we constantly voice our incapabilities and inadequacies, we are going to act in that line. For example, if you always say to yourself, "I suck at public speaking," that thought fills your mind with uncontrollable anxiety when you need to address a group of people. The result often is making a mess of the whole presentation. Your life doesn't become better that way. That's why you must be deliberate about the words you say.

Negative affirmations are just the opposite of positive affirmations. When you invest so many thoughts in the negative, your confidence starts to drain. The only way you fight this evil is by reaffirming the truth you want to materialize in your life.

THE SCIENCE BEHIND AFFIRMATIONS

The idea behind positive affirmations is that you can develop strong and pragmatic beliefs by reciting specific words repeatedly.

If you say something enough times to yourself, you'll start believing it. Repeating positive beliefs or thoughts to yourself conditions your brains to start thinking in that direction.

But many people wonder if science does support these claims.

The answer to that is YES.

SCIENTIFIC INVESTIGATIONS ON POSITIVE AFFIRMATIONS

Why do scientists believe that positive affirmations work?

Researchers have carried out different studies to test the effects of affirmations on the brain. If repeating words causes any change in the brain, we have every right to believe affirmations work. Interesting stuff, right?

In a study published in *Social Cognitive and Affective Neuroscience*, researchers Christopher Cascio and Emily Falk landed on a gold mine.

Here's what they discovered:

"Positive affirmations stimulated key reward centers in the brain."

These brain areas, particularly the ventral striatum and ventromedial prefrontal cortex, are the very centers activated by pleasure and satisfaction.

What that means is that positive affirmations work on our brain reward circuits, controlling our response to experiences and situations.

Therefore, with affirmations, we have control over threatening or negative information that comes to us.

As we repeat these affirmations and identify with them, we develop a positive thought pattern that eventually produces the right behavior and rewarding lifestyle that we desire.

BENEFITS OF POSITIVE AFFIRMATIONS

Successful black women like Oprah Winfrey and Viola Davis are prominent preachers of positive affirmations. It's evident that positive self-talk has produced incredible results in their lives.

You are next in line!

With positive affirmations, you can achieve the following:

• Erase negative thought patterns

• Boost your mood, confidence, and self-worth

• Gain motivation for an enriching life

• Unlock amazing potentials and possibilities

• Fill your life with boundless success

• Live a life of happiness and fulfillment

BEFORE YOU START your affirmations session, make sure you're comfortable and relaxed. Affirmations are best absorbed right when you wake up or before going to sleep. However, you can also listen to affirmations during the day, for example, when taking a walk.

If you enjoy this book and would like to help others improve their lives as well, please consider leaving a review. I personally read each and every review and love every time I come across a new one. Thank you!

I hope the affirmations in this book makes a difference in your life just as it did mine and many others. Best of luck!

CHAPTER 2
AFFIRMATIONS

1. I am full of positive energy and confidence.
2. I have enough courage to take on my goals and achieve my dreams.
3. I am happy today, tomorrow, and every day of my life.
4. No situations, life circumstances, or challenges can bring me down.
5. Yes, today is my day.
6. I love myself with everything I've got.
7. I wear my uniqueness as a badge.
8. There are no hurdles that I can't cross.
9. Every day is an opportunity to do it better, an opportunity to become a better version of myself.
10. I am a strong black woman.

11. I am a beautiful black woman, and I embrace respect, love, and kindness.
12. I deserve all the good things that show up in my life.
13. My self-worth doesn't depend on society's definition of me.
14. Life is an exciting journey for me.
15. My hair texture is perfect and beautiful, just the way it is.
16. I esteem myself as invaluable
17. My self-worth does not need the validation of people outside my body.
18. When I look at myself, beauty is all I see.
19. Today is another day to live the incredible life I desire.
20. I have complete control over my feelings and happiness.
21. Every day I get better than I was the previous day.
22. I have the power to create all the change I want to see.
23. I attract the right people into my life.
24. I surround myself with people that contribute to my growth and the advancement of my dreams.
25. I hold the keys to my happiness.

26. Everything will work out exactly the way it's supposed to.
27. What they think of me is irrelevant; the only important thing is what I think of myself.
28. I am beautiful, courageous, and daring.
29. I am made of the strength of ten thousand moons.
30. Life's tough, but I'm tougher.
31. I inhale positive energy and get rid of every negative energy.
32. I am proud of who I am - limitless, beautiful, and wonderful.
33. I let go of all anxiety, depression, and attachments.
34. I let go of unforgiveness, grudges, and malice.
35. I am worthy of all the happiness in the world.
36. I am full of happiness.
37. I am getting stronger and bigger than every limitation.
38. I win by staying true to myself.
39. I attract the right people into my life.
40. My self-worth is high beyond what people think of me.
41. I walk in clarity of purpose in my relationships, business, and career.
42. I am loving, lovable, and loved.

43. My black skin is radiant and beautiful.
44. I am all out to do great things.
45. I know I have the capabilities to achieve mind-blowing success.
46. I take advantage of every opportunity and challenge that comes my way.
47. Shrinkage has no place in me.
48. Failure has no place in my life.
49. I heal from every pain, hurt, and disappointment.
50. The past remains in the past as I walk into the future with all optimism.
51. I'm not boxed into the corner of despair and regret.
52. I am energetically drawn to all the things I deserve.
53. When I walk into a room, my energy is palpable.
54. I am more than enough.
55. I love my body.
56. The strength of my character doesn't lie in the color of my skin.
57. I am one hundred percent comfortable in my skin.
58. I am proud of who I am and of everything I continue to accomplish.

59. I have a firm grip on life.

60. There's no confusion around me.

61. I achieve my goals one at a time, and I'm never distracted.

62. Everything around me is working and producing astounding results.

63. My relationships flourish.

64. I'm not held back by the hurts I've suffered.

65. I'm steeped into loving and being loved by the right people.

66. I may not have all the answers I need, but I know I'm headed in the right direction.

67. I take responsibility for my happiness.

68. I have complete control over what I feel and how I feel.

69. I embrace the wonder and magic inside of me.

70. I surround myself with amazing people that provide support and encouragement.

71. Every decision I make brings me immense happiness.

72. Success comes to me quickly and effortlessly.

73. My income is ever-growing.

74. I attract enough money and financial resources into my life.

75. I choose to live an enriching life.

76. I think sufficiency, not scarcity.
77. I have all I need, when I need it, and where I need it.
78. I make the right investments for my financial prosperity.
79. I am comfortable standing my ground and not breaking under pressure.
80. I have complete confidence in my decisions.
81. Brilliance and excellence are the adjectives that describe me.
82. I am strong, powerful, and courageous.
83. I do not go with the labels the society puts on me. Instead, I herald my own definition.
84. I am a shining and burning light.
85. Nothing from my past draws me back or cages me in one corner.
86. I go through life with all optimism and positivity.
87. Regardless of the situation, I think positive thoughts.
88. Regardless of the situation, I speak positive words.
89. Regardless of the situation, I take positive actions.
90. Regardless of the situation, I maintain a positive attitude.

91. If I want it, I can work hard to get it.
92. Nothing's beyond my reach.
93. My body is beautiful.
94. My mind never lacks good and enriching ideas.
95. I have the strength, motivation, and resources to turn my ideas into great results.
96. I am not carefree or complacent about my dreams.
97. I am set out for greatness, and there's nothing stopping me.
98. I know I am more than good enough, regardless of what society says.
99. I know I am intelligent and smart, regardless of people's opinions.
100. I am ready to get out of my comfort zone and explore the boundless opportunities that abound out there.
101. Nothing will ever take away my gratitude for the beautiful things and people that I have.
102. I stay on top of every situation.
103. My life is an inspiration to those around me.
104. I have the power to decide how I respond to every situation.
105. My words are always positive, confident, and life-giving.

106. People are comfortable around me.
107. I am not suspicious, judgmental, and condemning.
108. I believe in the very best of people.
109. My heart is set at the default of forgiveness.
110. I am a caring, forgiving, and kind black woman.
111. I am a passionate and purpose-driven black woman.
112. I am a sweet and amiable black woman.
113. Pleasantness surrounds me, and I radiate pleasantness.
114. Goodness and favor surround me.
115. I am a successful and prosperous black woman.
116. I am excited to take on the challenges that life brings.
117. I am grateful for every experience I've had to go through.
118. I look forward to facing life with so much courage.
119. I am grateful for all my relationships.
120. I appreciate all the wonderful people that I have around me.
121. No, I don't give up. Quitting isn't an option.
122. My words are always uplifting.

123. Today is the best day ever, and I absorb all the beauty in it.

124. My skin not only radiates beauty, my heart radiates kindness.

125. I am helpful and resourceful.

126. As I step into today, I remind everyone how valuable I am.

127. I create and enjoy the life that I am proud of.

128. When I put my heart into a task, I see it to the finish line.

129. I get better at what I do.

130. I get the best result out of everything I do.

131. My children are proud of the mother that I am to them.

132. I have a supportive family.

133. I understand the specific needs of my family, and I do my best to address them.

134. I am not insensitive to the pain of others.

135. While I prioritize my happiness, I don't neglect the happiness of those around me.

136. I make the life of others better.

137. My speech is seasoned, and my words are always comforting.

138. I love the Black Queen that I am.

139. My values and habits are in sync with my goals and aspirations.

140. I let go of every negative programming and mindset.

141. I am a walking example of Black beauty and excellence.

142. I maintain a clear mind and disposition in the face of conflicts. I make the right decisions that calm the storm.

143. I chose to radiate love. It doesn't matter the negativity outside there.

144. My heart is pure. My intentions are pure.

145. I am not obsessed with any idea that I need to impress others. I have absolutely nothing to prove to anyone.

146. I let go of everything that adds no value to my life.

147. From now on, I only focus on things that serve a need in my life.

148. I am worthy of being celebrated.

149. I am unique in every way.

150. I honor my uniqueness.

151. In every situation, I choose happiness.

152. I am beautiful inside and out.

153. I love, cherish, and appreciate myself.

154. I have the power to create my reality, and that's exactly what I do everyday.

155. I am not bitter, resentful, or vengeful.

Instead, I am kind, patient, and forgiving.

156. I don't compare myself to other people. I work by my own standards.

157. Every day, I get better than yesterday.

158. I take full responsibility for my actions and always strive to do better.

159. I take care of my body.

160. I eat the right foods, foods that nourish my body.

161. I rest when I need to.

162. I don't overload my mind with unproductive and negative thoughts.

163. I am in complete control of my thoughts at all times.

164. I am more than committed to my own success.

165. My life is as beautiful as I want it to be.

166. I exceed expectations in my career and business.

167. I love myself unconditionally.

168. People's words won't decide how much I value my body.

169. I don't derive my sense of self-worth from the words of others.

170. I am as beautiful as I can ever be.

171. I am conscious of all the positive qualities that I possess.
172. It doesn't matter how many times I fail. I am getting back up.
173. I succeed in leadership positions.
174. This career is mine for the taking.
175. I take bold steps to the actualization of my career plans.
176. I am forever committed to making my life work. I am not giving up.
177. I am stronger than my excuses.
178. I trust my inner voice.
179. I know how to navigate through life.
180. I am a testament to the greatness of black women.
181. I am a rich, beautiful, and successful black woman.
182. My thoughts, opinions, and ideas are just as important as anyone else's.
183. I love myself more than anything else.
184. I am beautiful inside and out.
185. There's nothing that I need that I can not have.
186. I attract all the good things in life.
187. My gender places no limitations on me.
188. I love being a black woman.

189. I am strong in character, tough in resilience.
190. There's no giving up in my consciousness.
191. There's no diversion from my goals and dreams.
192. I am proud of my ambitions.
193. I am unapologetic of my convictions and I herald them with all confidence.
194. I make good and quality decisions.
195. My decisions make my life better.
196. I am wary of making the wrong decisions.
197. I flourish in every career step that I take.
198. Today is another day to put a smile on my face and on the faces of those around me.
199. I do not have a better yesterday.
200. My optimism for the future is unparalleled.
201. I honor my existence by living a life of purpose.
202. I celebrate my uniqueness and I won't lose myself to be someone else.
203. The best person to be is myself.
204. I honor myself.
205. I have complete control over my emotions.
206. I have complete control over my words.
207. I have complete control over my decisions.
208. I enjoy the journey of life and I embrace happiness all the way.

209. I do not succumb to fear and rejections.

210. I am a magnet for favor and blessings.

211. I approach life with an open mind, ready to explore the uniqueness of my world.

212. I am a magnet for life-changing opportunities.

213. I repel negative emotions.

214. My heart does not harbor bitterness and wrath.

215. I do not hoard unhealthy thoughts in my mind.

216. I only think pure thoughts.

217. Generational trauma does not serve me, so I let it go.

218. I remain calm in the most turbulent of storms.

219. I overcome anxiety. It does me no good.

220. I overcome despair. It serves no purpose in my life.

221. I overcome depression. It is not mine.

222. I refuse to be entitled to what's not mine.

223. I choose to forgive.

224. I let go of guilt, shame, and anger.

225. I embrace myself.

226. I am not ashamed of who I am.

227. My past has no say in my present and future.

228. I see everyday as an opportunity to build.
229. I do not weep beside the rubble of failed plans. Instead, I start to rebuild.
230. I learn from every situation and make better decisions.
231. I am a brilliant black woman capable of making the right decisions.
232. I am stronger than I appear.
233. I am comfortable in my black skin.
234. I am filled with love, joy, and content.
235. I am content with all I have, yet I reach for more.
236. I embrace wealth and abundance.
237. I embrace forgiveness.
238. I embrace letting go of the past.
239. I have a positive body image.
240. My body is alive and vibrant.
241. My body screams of energy and vitality.
242. The entire universe works for my health, wellbeing, and success.
243. I am not comfortable with failure.
244. I am worthy of never-ending success. So I'm ever committed to achieving great success.
245. I do not lose sight of the beautiful people I have around me.
246. I am grateful for all the support I get.

247. I am the emblem of greatness.
248. My effort and commitment bring success.
249. I am resilient in pursuing my success.
250. I am proud of my accomplishments.
251. I am grateful for all the success I have achieved.
252. My life is important to the world.
253. My skills and resources are important.
254. I am abundant in nature.
255. I flourish in energy.
256. I shine in the darkest of places.
257. I live, move, and have my being in love.
258. Love is all around me.
259. Love is inside of me.
260. I am an effervescence of love - today, tomorrow, and forever.
261. My whole life is loving and lovely.
262. I attract love every I go.
263. I am important.
264. I am full of kindness, love, and compassion.
265. I see being kind to others as being kind to myself.
266. I serve my community with humility.
267. My life is spent for the good of my community and society.
268. My life is hope to those in despair.

269. My life is courage to the faint-hearted.

270. My life is an inspiration to those who are downtrodden.

271. My life radiates hope, courage, and optimism.

272. I am a woman that knows her worth.

273. I am a woman that takes pride in her integrity, accomplishments, and abilities.

274. I am blessed with an abundance of gifts and I am not hesitant about sharing them.

275. My gifts are for the benefit of mankind.

276. I am selfless - as selfless as I could possibly be.

277. I share my gifts with the world.

278. I bring light to the world.

279. I bring life to the world.

280. My potential is limitless and I manifest it.

281. My love is limitless and I show it.

282. My life is limitless and I express it.

283. My ability is boundless and I embrace it.

284. I receive an unlimited source of financial abundance into my life.

285. I have more than enough money.

286. All the money I spend come back to me in multiple folds.

287. I always make the right financial decisions.

288. I trust my faculties to make the right investment decisions.

289. I do not get into the cycle of debts.

290. I can see danger a thousand miles away.

291. I embrace multiple sources of income.

292. I am blessed immeasurably.

293. I receive undeserved blessings into my life.

294. I am the creator of my reality.

295. My future is right in my hands.

296. I am my biggest motivator.

297. I am worthy of my desires. I am worthy of my dreams.

298. I am spiritually strong, mentally focused, and physically free.

299. I allow nothing to bother me.

300. I am not a slave to anything.

301. I allow nothing to break me.

302. I refuse to bow down to pressure.

303. I have more than enough energy for the vibrant life I want to live.

304. I am in charge of my destiny.

305. The fulfillment of my destiny is important to the world.

306. The world awaits my breakthrough.

307. I refuse to fail my world.

308. I am living my dreams.

309. I find satisfaction in the happiness of others.

310. I refuse to be jealous of the success of another.
311. I refuse to be envious of someone else.
312. I celebrate the victories of my friends and family.
313. I contribute genuinely to the success of people around me.
314. I do everything with utmost genuineness.
315. All I offer is love.
316. I give the best of myself every day.
317. I am wholeness.
318. There's nothing lacking in me.
319. I break free from every idea that imprisons me.
320. I am on the right path to success.
321. I refuse to be distracted from my goals.
322. I continue to cheer myself on.
323. It is a blessing to attain this success.
324. It is a blessing to have so much to look forward to.
325. My life is so full of bliss.
326. My life's journey is filled with excitement and bliss.
327. My life is full of compassion and love.
328. My past does not define me.
329. I am full of boundless love.

330. My mind is capable of incredible innovations.
331. I am beautiful and perfect as I am.
332. I believe in myself every day.
333. My offering to the world is love and the gift of myself.
334. I am dependable and trustworthy.
335. My friends depend on me.
336. I am a reliable person.
337. I learn to keep my word and honor agreement.
338. I am relevant to everyone around me.
339. I find satisfaction in fulfilling my purpose.
340. My blessings are incalculable.
341. It doesn't matter what other people think, being a black woman is a unique experience.
342. I am emotionally available to my loved ones.
343. I am open, receptive, and attentive.
344. My mind remains focused on my goals.
345. I only dwell on good, healthy, and beneficial thoughts.
346. I have peace of mind.
347. My experience as a black woman is one of positivity.
348. My experience as a black woman is filled with tranquility.

349. My experience as a black woman is a beautiful tale.

350. I am productive in every area of my life.

351. I am beautiful on the inside and out.

352. I am intelligent and creative.

353. My ideas are worthy of being heard.

354. I permit myself to be full of vitality.

355. I am blessed.

356. I breathe in fulfillment and breathe out joy.

357. I have the ability to sustain all that is valuable to me.

358. I retain my joy.

359. I am happy always, regardless of the situation I face.

360. Everything around me is working together for my good.

361. My heart has enough strength to keep me going in the journey of life.

362. My voice will be heard in every room.

363. I find a seat at any table I want to sit.

364. I refuse to dwell on offenses. Instead I serenade my heart with forgiveness.

365. I have the ability to forgive even those that are undeserving.

366. I forgive people for my own happiness and peace.

367. I prioritize my peace of mind above everything else.

368. I pay close attention to my body and health.

369. I take care of my body and give it all it deserves.

370. I embrace good health for my body and mind.

371. My mind is alert and alive.

372. I have boundless prosperity.

373. I am wealthier than I ever thought I could be.

374. My mind is a factory of productive thoughts.

375. My mind is immersed in harmony and tranquility.

376. I bring peace to everyone around me.

377. I tower above every obstacle in my way.

378. I find a way around even the most difficult of situations.

379. I find an answer to the most complex of problems.

380. I receive adequate answers to all my questions about life.

381. As I step out today, each and every one of my activities is enriching.

382. I appreciate time and use every minute I have with prudence.

383. I value every moment.

384. I make the best out of every opportunity.

385. There is no scarcity of opportunities for me.

386. I am boundless and limitless.

387. I am amazing and invaluable.

388. I know how to keep and grow relationships.

389. I embrace letting go of my ego for the good of my relationships.

390. I embrace accepting my faults and working on myself to become better.

391. I become better every day.

392. I am mentally healthy.

393. This is the strongest I have ever been.

394. This is the healthiest I have ever been.

395. I have remarkable strength.

396. I feel alive with every breath that I take.

397. I have the right mental attitude to approach life's dynamics.

398. My opinions and ideas are as valid as everyone else's.

399. I am safe.

400. I refuse to take second place when I can be the first.

401. I have a winning mentality.

402. My hard work matches my winning mentality.

403. I put in the right work for the results I desire.

404. I am mentally capable for the challenges that come my way.

405. I am not limited in any way by the color of my skin.

406. I know how to turn challenges into opportunities.

407. I am strong and perfect.

408. I am dedicated and committed to my goals.

409. My commitment and dedication inspire people around me.

410. I am soft.

411. I am worthy of my biggest dreams coming true.

412. My energy attracts the right people to my life effortlessly.

413. My life is full of people that love and appreciate me.

414. I am immeasurably loved.

415. Love is a common, but valuable commodity in my life.

416. I find it easy to love people.

417. I find it easy to reach out to people.

418. I find it easy to lend a helping hand.

419. I find it easy to be a blessing to people.

420. I have an endless supply of energy.

421. I refused to be caged by any beauty standards. I define my own standards.

422. I am as beautiful as I ever can be.

423. I am as amazing as I ever can be.

424. I am as confident as I ever can be.

425. I shape my life with positive thoughts.

426. My words are encouraging and uplifting.

427. I embrace patience and contentment.

428. I learn to make decisions that are just perfect for me.

429. I appreciate the immense help I have around me.

430. I am a great mother. I am a wonderful partner. I am an amazing sister.

431. I am a dependable friend. I am a pleasant colleague. I am a friendly neighbor.

432. I embrace freedom in my thoughts and ideas.

433. I reprogram my mind with positive thoughts.

434. Positivity spreads from my thoughts to my words and then to my actions.

435. I reprogram my subconscious mind to align with my dreams.

436. I am not bound by stereotypes and beauty standards.

437. I overcome self-sabotage by believing the right things about me.

438. I refuse every negative narration about the black woman.
439. I am a powerful woman.
440. I am strength.
441. I am energized for every task I have to accomplish.
442. I am worthy regardless of my past circumstances.
443. I am beyond my shortcomings.
444. I am better than my inadequacies.
445. I understand my purpose in life.
446. I stay focused on my path of purpose.
447. I have unlimited opportunities.
448. Everyone around me supports my dreams and aspirations.
449. I receive the necessary support to make my dreams come true.
450. I receive adequate emotional support.
451. I open my heart to love and be loved.
452. I deserve love, care, and attention.
453. My spirit is unbreakable, even in the fiercest of storms.
454. My non-conformity to unrealistic beauty standards takes nothing away from me.
455. I am proud of my truth and convictions.

456. I have the right to hold and express my opinions.

457. My mind is capable of forming informed opinions.

458. I define who I am and what I am capable of.

459. I create more success in my life.

460. There's no limit to the things I can accomplish.

461. If I set my heart to it, I can do it.

462. I develop the habits of highly effective people.

463. I maintain the habits of successful people.

464. I refuse to fall into the web of procrastination.

465. I do what I am supposed to do, when I am supposed to do it, and how I am supposed to do it.

466. Excellence is my creed in every single thing I do.

467. I only accept things that bring blessings into my life.

468. I value peace over conflict.

469. My entire body is aligned to my goal.

470. I am self-sufficient

471. I have enough strength on my inside to always draw from.

472. The whole universe supports my being.

473. My existence is a blessing to the entire universe.
474. I prefer to blind the world with my brilliance than please it with my dimness.
475. My true value does not lie in the physical things I possess.
476. I am grateful for every blessing that comes into my life.
477. I have enough room for more blessings.
478. I am only content with excellence.
479. The world may settle for mediocrity but my heart is set on excellence.
480. I choose to be a good person.
481. I choose to be a kind person.
482. I have the power to choose how to react to every action done to me.
483. I have the power to choose how I feel about something.
484. My sense of self-worth appreciates.
485. I place premium on myself.
486. I am a creative genius - anytime, any day.
487. My black is beautiful and I refuse to accept every stereotypical assertion.
488. When it comes to me, I define the terms.
489. When it comes to me, I decide what's acceptable.

490. I have complete control over my personal space.
491. I have control over the thoughts that dominate my mind.
492. I acknowledge and manage the influences around me.
493. I only accept positive influences.
494. I can say NO and stand by my word.
495. I am firm, resolute, and uncompromising.
496. I only compare myself with myself.
497. I defend what I believe in.
498. I stand by my truth and I pull everyone around me to understand this truth.
499. I am willing to be the only woman in the room to stand for what I believe in.
500. I deserve a seat at the best tables.
501. When I fail at something I give it another try.
502. My only destination is success; every other thing is a process.
503. I remain passionate about my dreams, regardless of how long it takes.
504. I am a courageous black woman who believes in her dreams.
505. Health and wellness is for me.
506. I move from one ladder of breakthrough to another.

507. There is room for me at the very top.

508. I overcome weariness and despair.

509. I am content with my abilities and I continue to bring out the best of them.

510. Good things are coming my way.

511. I become a better person every day.

512. There's no single problem I face without a solution.

513. My challenges contribute to my growth.

514. My mistakes are opportunities for me to learn and grow.

515. I am a good leader.

516. I surround myself with people who love and cherish me.

517. I have people who honor and respect me.

518. I have one hundred percent confidence in my dreams.

519. I am perfectly okay with not knowing everything.

520. I make the best out of every information I get.

521. I choose to think it is possible.

522. Doors open to me.

523. I can survive anything and come out better.

524. I am capable of incredible things.

525. I am capable of whatever challenges I have to face.

526. My mind stays focused.

527. I excel in whatever I seek to do.

528. I give myself the freedom and liberty to explore the world.

529. I make immense contributions to my workplace.

530. I carry about an aura of self-worth and confidence.

531. I speak my desires every day and I see them come to pass.

532. I have enough money to do all the things I want to do.

533. I am exceptional.

534. I take charge of my future and everything that happens in it.

535. I am confident that everything is going to work out fine.

536. I am courageous enough to step out of my comfort zone.

537. I receive the rewards of my hard work and labor.

538. I know things can only get better.

539. I am assured of a better tomorrow.

540. Today is going to be a fantastic day.

541. Today is going to be filled with so many blessings and opportunities.
542. I step out today with so much courage to face life.
543. I succeed at everything I desire to do.
544. I have all it takes to meet my needs.
545. My results surpass my expectations.
546. I get better in my behavior and attitude.
547. I am a pleasant soul.
548. I get better in my relationships.
549. I find it easy to begin and sustain a conversation.
550. I know the right things to say.
551. I am an interesting and exciting black woman.
552. I choose to live beyond labels that seek to limit me.
553. I see myself through my very eyes, not through the eyes of society.
554. I am a pacesetter.
555. I am a trailblazer.
556. Things improve every step of the way.
557. I rise above the most difficult of circumstances.
558. I cultivate habits that improve my life.

559. I imbibe good hygiene and habits that improve my health.

560. Every system in my body cooperates with my dream of lifelong success.

561. I am filled with all the vitality I need to go through life.

562. I am a conqueror. I am a victor.

563. Circumstances bow to my resilience.

564. Situations bow to my courage.

565. Hurdles crumble before my resilience.

566. I keep to the ideas I strongly believe in. No giving up.

567. My brain is quick to grab information and does well to retain it.

568. I am smarter than I could possibly be.

569. Today, I choose to be happy and positive.

570. Today, I choose to wear a smile and be pleasant.

571. Today, I choose to leave behind my struggles with inadequacies.

572. I am strong enough to work on my inadequacies and become a better person.

573. I give my body the right exercises it needs.

574. I prioritize my health over temporary desire for pleasure and satisfaction.

575. Exercises are profitable to my health and well-being.

576. I acknowledge that the long-term sustenance of my body depends on my everyday habits.

577. I have complete control of my day-to-day habits.

578. My idiosyncrasies are not hurtful to people around me.

579. I put up a cheerful attitude every time.

580. I choose cheerfulness over sadness.

581. I am the most vibrant person I know.

582. I am the most positive person I know.

583. My focus is on the beautiful things about me.

584. I am a magnet of financial success.

585. I am whole as a black woman. There's no missing piece in me.

586. My steps are always going forward.

587. I count every day as an opportunity to make things better.

588. I refuse to worry about things I have no control over.

589. I refuse to fill my mind with thoughts that add no value to me.

590. I refuse to harbor relationships that hurt me.

591. I embrace saying "no" to hurtful relationships.

592. I own my truth.

593. I choose to create a unique story for myself.

594. I know how to articulate my points.

595. Communication is not a problem for me.

596. I know the right words to say in every situation.

597. Patiently, I will work my way to the top.

598. I refuse to take no for an answer.

599. I am a strong-willed black woman with a purpose.

600. The content of my character defines me more than anything else.

601. I value my opinion about myself above what anyone else has to say.

602. I listen to and appreciate honest feedback.

603. I embrace a culture of honest review and critique.

604. I accept that there are people around me who mean my good.

605. I have good, loving, and loyal friends.

606. I have very supportive friends.

607. I am grateful for the amazing friendships I have in my life.

608. I feel supported all along the way.

609. I am not alone. I have people who care about me in this journey of life.

610. I appreciate people's effort to make me better.

611. I am grateful for the gifts of people.

612. I work in a healthy environment.

613. The culture in my workplace promotes productivity.

614. I am a fantastic team-player.

615. I learn to listen to others, share ideas, and work together.

616. I am a pleasant person to be with.

617. It's okay to make mistakes.

618. I learn to make the right choices.

619. I work at my own pace.

620. I am proud of the decisions I make.

621. I surround myself with positive and optimistic people.

622. My breakthrough is just around the corner.

623. I know I am going to be very successful.

624. I know I am going to live a life my children will be proud of.

625. I know my life will not be a waste.

626. I know I am going to dwell in riches and prosperity.

627. I spread positivity all around me.

628. I spread love everywhere I go.

629. I break free of stereotypes and I lead an amazing life.

630. Today is my day.

631. Today is going to be a beautiful day.

632. People around me support my positive habits.

633. I have the commitment to stay true to my resolutions.

634. I approach life with passion and drive.

635. I feel stronger and better with every breath I take.

636. My black is radiant and beautiful.

637. I am going out today to do great things.

638. Nothing is impossible to me.

639. I am rich. I am successful. I am everything I've always wanted to be.

640. I am grateful for today.

641. I have the strength to pull through today and every other day that comes.

642. Nothing is worth losing my happiness for.

643. My happiness is completely up to me.

644. I choose to let go of every painful feeling and memory.

645. I am a better person everyday.

646. I attract joy and happiness into my life.

647. I am open to possibilities that lead to a greater purpose.

648. I think in abundance, not lack.

649. Today is a new day to start afresh.

650. I evolve with my purpose every single day.

651. I am overwhelmed with positive energy.

652. I love my skin.

653. I realize that I am fit and capable.

654. I respect the journey of others.

655. I refuse to choose less for myself.

656. I demand the best of myself.

657. I engage with brilliant minds in my daily conversations.

658. I feel privileged to have amazing people around me.

659. I channel my energy to things that really matter.

660. It's okay to take breaks on my way to the success I desire.

661. I am enough. I do enough. I have enough.

662. People appreciate what I have to offer.

663. I enjoy my work. I love my career.

664. I am not controlled by the expectations of others.

665. I am making a mark on this world.

666. I was born for a purpose.

667. My life is amazing. I was born for this.

668. I create value that helps others lead a more enriching life.

669. Everything around me is flourishing.

670. I am unique. I am original. I am authentic.

671. I always have an abundance of ideas.

672. I deserve every dollar I earn.

673. I give myself permission to make mistakes.

674. I give myself permission to do what is best for me.

675. I am full of brilliant ideas.

676. My very existence makes a difference in the world.

677. I follow my dreams passionately.

678. I let go of every resentment in my heart.

679. I have all the qualities of a successful person.

680. I handle stuff easily.

681. I let go of the things that no longer serve me.

682. I refuse to give up.

683. I continue to explore all options available to me.

684. I refuse to let my weaknesses make the headline.

685. I am passionate about a noble cause.

686. I am a free woman.

687. I am not a slave to my past, to my fears, to rejections.

688. My life is a splendid one and I'm enjoying every bit of it.

689. I am an inspiration to my world.

690. I am getting the results that I have long dreamed of.

691. My life is made beautiful by the decisions I make.

692. I conquer my fears and doubts. I go all out with courage.

693. I tower above my circumstances.

694. I attract positive situations that lead to success.

695. I am grateful for the immense ability that I have to achieve my goals.

696. I am prepared to take advantage of every opportunity that comes my way.

697. I know when to walk away.

698. I am able to cultivate the life I enjoy.

699. I do not compete for attention.

700. I want to be remembered as someone who lived a life she enjoyed.

701. I have the wisdom to handle life challenges

702. I have the courage to solve the biggest issues in my face

703. I am ready for what the future holds for me

704. I am a better woman than I was yesterday

705. I know how to handle my finances

706. I do not make terrible financial decisions

707. I do not live in a cycle of debts

708. No one lacks around me because I am a generous person

709. Every business idea I touch turns into gold

710. I am not desperate for people's attention or validation

711. My life is an embodiment of success and breakthroughs

712. I do not repeat the mistakes of yesterday. I learn from them and make better decisions.

713. Physical possessions do not define my true worth

714. I draw strength from the fact that I have all it takes to achieve my goals

715. I am not affected by stereotypes out there

716. My mind is sound and not beclouded with indecision and fear

717. I am the most brilliant person that I know

718. Today is going to be the most successful day of my life

719. Today means I have another opportunity to get the job done

720. I don't give up easily

721. I see my goals to the end

722. My days are filled with bliss and vitality

723. I am an exemplary black woman — in my workplace, neighborhood, and society

724. I refuse to be a disappointment to my children
725. I am a source of inspiration to many
726. Being a black woman is not a disadvantage in any way
727. I turn my challenges into opportunities for outstanding success
728. My life has purpose and direction
729. I am a visionary black woman
730. I have a steadfast love for my job
731. My dedication to my life's goals is a great motivation to those around me
732. I choose to live the best life I can while I yet breathe
733. Even when things don't go my way, I find a reason to be happy
734. Even when things don't do as they should, I find a way to stay motivated
735. I don't give up after my first try
736. I believe in the power of consistency and persistence
737. I am a positive person all year round
738. I take responsibility for my actions and work hard to improve them
739. I do not blame others for the mistakes I make
740. I am a responsible black woman

741. I am in for the best life has to offer
742. I have the patience to work with different kinds of people
743. I am not intolerant and discriminatory
744. I see the best in people, no matter their shortcomings
745. My life is a whole new wonder to behold
746. I am a source of encouragement to those in despair
747. My life is fruitful; there's no dryness anywhere
748. I'm entirely at peace with where I am now while I reach out for more
749. No matter how hopeless the situation seems, I'll always find my way out
750. When darkness looms, I shine brighter than ever
751. I am a trustworthy and reliable black woman
752. I take pride in my womanhood
753. I am not ashamed to stand up tall as a black woman
754. I soar above every hurdle on my way and refuse to take the backseat
755. I don't quit when it gets tough; instead, I rise stronger than ever before

756. My mind has the ability to keep it all together when everything seems to be falling apart

757. I am ready to accept the victory that's coming my way

758. I'm not lazy; I'm not lousy, I'm not careless

759. I have unique talents and abilities that set me apart from the crowd

760. When I look back at today in years to come, I'm going to be proud of the decisions I made

761. I am carefully creating a desirable future for myself and my kids

762. I know when to take a break and give my body the rest it needs

763. I know how to live a healthy lifestyle

764. I know how to care for my body

765. I recognize how essential thoughts are, and I don't entertain negative thoughts

766. My mind is filled with positive thoughts all day long

767. I trust my resolution to live a fulfilling life

768. The whole universe is working in my favor

769. Today I will have a good heart

770. I am committed to making a positive change by doing new things

771. I will not apologize for being a confident black woman

772. I rise above all judgments of my skin color
773. I support my peers in their goals
774. I offer the most brilliant ideas in the room
775. I create a life that I am completely proud of
776. Nothing is ever going to take me to place of depression and despair
777. I am fully in control of my thought process, and I only allow life-giving thoughts
778. I do not form my opinions from the place of hurt and bitterness
779. I excel in the place of forgiveness
780. No offense is greater than my peace of mind
781. Healthy living starts with right eating, so I stay away from junk
782. My body is strong, fit, and healthy
783. I'm in the best shape of health right now
784. I'm resilient towards my health and fitness goals
785. My success story inspires others to achieve great success
786. I deserve all these fabulous things that are coming into my life
787. I deserve all these amazing friendships that I have
788. This is my opportunity, and I am going to take it

789. I make the best of the opportunities that come my way today
790. My work deserves admiration and respect
791. I do not let fear cage me in a corner
792. I go all out to achieve the success I desire
793. I am blessed immeasurably
794. I am a savvy businesswoman
795. I make intelligent business decisions
796. I reprogram my mind for success and prosperity
797. I am intentional about my success
798. Every day, I know what I'm supposed to do
799. I understand my purpose of being here
800. I am motivated to succeed
801. Everything that I do promotes my goals without affecting others
802. I trust my intuition
803. I have the purpose of doing incredible things
804. I am a loving partner to my equally-loving partner
805. I don't let the feeling of fear hold me back
806. No area of my life lacks success
807. There's nothing capable of stopping me
808. Everything is good around me
809. I value and honor myself

810. My relationship serves a good purpose in my life

811. I attract prosperity every single day

812. I am the most influential person in my own life

813. I allow others to be themselves

814. I accept the things that I cannot change, and I don't worry about them

815. I build the foundation of my life and choose what stays in it

816. I am far above low actions

817. I only surround myself with positivity

818. My positivity attracts good people into my life

819. I am charming

820. I replace anger and bitterness with love

821. I trust myself to build a fantastic future

822. I love knowledge

823. I am open-minded and willing to learn new things

824. I am satisfied with my own company

825. I am positive, regardless of the negativity that surrounds me

826. I am the best I can be in my work

827. I am resilient and hardworking

828. I am worthy of prosperity

829. I am creative
830. I am quick to forgive
831. I learn to forgive people for their wrongdoings
832. There are no stagnant days in my life
833. I am always making progress
834. My words don't cause pain or hurt to others
835. I learn to treat people kindly and compassionately
836. In my relationship with others, compassion is my watchword
837. I care for my body like my life depends on it because it actually does
838. I make the right decisions for a healthy and fulfilling life
839. I do not give up too soon
840. I have the winner's mentality

NOTES

NOTES

NOTES

NOTES

Milton Keynes UK
Ingram Content Group UK Ltd.
UKHW041849250923
429376UK00001B/11

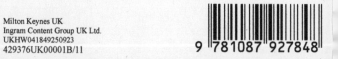

9 781087 927848